TONY EVANS
SPEAKS OUT ON
GAMBLING
AND THE
LOTTERY

TONY EVANS
SPEAKS OUT ON
GAMBLING
AND THE
LOTTERY

MOODY PRESS
CHICAGO

All Scripture quotations are taken from the
New American Standard Bible, © 1960, 1962,
1963, 1968, 1971, 1972, 1973, 1975, and 1977
by The Lockman Foundation, and are used by
permission.

ISBN: 0-8024-2562-3

1 3 5 7 9 10 8 6 4 2

Printed in the United States of America

Steve had no reason to believe that Kate, his wife of sixteen years, was anything other than a devoted wife and mother of two: a boy and a girl, ages nine and eleven. Life for this family in Colleyville, Illinois, seemed pretty normal.

Kate did all the right things. She tatted lace, knitted scarves, and collected pig figurines. She was a volunteer at their local church. Maybe, just maybe, if it hadn't been for that one little excursion. . . .

Steve and Kate had decided to visit a casino to celebrate her fortieth birthday. They agreed ahead of time to control their gambling; they would spend no more than forty dollars. It was a nice birthday outing.

But something happened to Kate that night. Somehow, gambling caught her in its grip, even after just one experience. Unknown to Steve, Kate returned to gambling in a big way.

She stopped paying the house mortgage. She pawned her wedding rings, then his rings. She lost time and again, but she kept going back until she had quietly bankrupted the family.

Finally, Kate was notified by a process server and officials from the sheriff's office that the bank was foreclosing on their home. The family would have to move.

That morning, she drove her children to school. Back at home, she took a pistol from the basement desk drawer. She wrote a note, addressed "to whom it may concern." She drove to a nearby parking lot, crawled into the backseat of her car, and shot herself in the head. The shame and embarrassment were too much for her.

Obviously, Steve said, she could not face him or their minister or anybody else about it. Later, he found a paper trail that read like a diary of Kate's hidden life aboard the gambling boats along the Mississippi River.

A spokesman for the casinos Kate frequented could only say that the company had posted signs in the casinos advertising Gamblers Anonymous. He said it would be impossible to keep track of every gambler, and that casinos let people know the risks when they come in.

Al's problem wasn't nearly as severe. He limited himself to a two-dollar daily bet on the horses at his local racetrack. The problem was, during several months of this period, Al was unemployed and his family had little to spare. As he said later, it may have been only two dollars a day, but it was money he didn't have to gamble with. He just couldn't resist.

Gambling is a complex and difficult subject to discuss because it has so many different levels and nuances and perceptions attached to it. But we'd better find out what God has to say about it because lives are at stake.

In a very generic sense, gambling is simply taking a risk. We do that in a lot of different ways. When you get up and go to church, you take a risk that you will not get there safely. When I go to amusement parks, I love to play the arcade games and try to win a bear. So I take a risk.

Investments in the stock market are a risk. You are gambling that your investments will go up and not down. You take a risk when you play the market.

This issue has become more complex since the advent of casinos, lotteries, and riverboat gambling. The question I get most often is, "Is it OK for Christians to play the lottery?" A related question I get as a pastor is, "Will the church accept an offering from the lottery money if I win?"

When I was growing up, things were a lot simpler. You gambled in one of a couple of ways. One of the things I did back in the "hood" in Baltimore was pitch pennies against the wall with the guys. The one closest to the wall won all the pennies. And then there was dice-rolling.

Some people considered games like Monopoly to be gambling. In fact, the church in which I grew up included people who would not allow any board games if dice were involved because that was viewed as gambling.

Maybe you picked up this booklet looking for a simple, all-inclusive answer, such as: Don't gamble, ever, in any form. But the question can't be answered that easily, because there's a lot involved. You see, from God's standpoint, all gambling isn't equal. Now that may sound surprising to you, but I will show you what I mean as we go along.

So rather than simply arguing whether to gamble or not to gamble, we need to understand the different types of gambling and find out what is acceptable to God and what is not. Many people don't know the difference.

Some Opening Observations

In this booklet we will look at ten crucial questions about gambling. I want to give you biblical guidance on the issue, but again the answers aren't always black-and-white. Now that does *not* mean God's Word is unclear on the basic issues. Not at all.

But once you have the biblical data, you must answer many of these questions for yourself. What I want to do is give you a biblical perspective so you can have a clear heart and conscience before God on these questions.

This is a serious issue, because more than one hundred million Americans gamble on some level. Three hundred billion dollars a year are spent on gambling. Whether it is playing cards in a friend's home, voting on a casino, or buying a lottery ticket at the corner market, gambling touches all of us at some point.

Let me make a couple preliminary observations before we go to the ten questions. Observation number one: *God is not against wealth per se.* Deuteronomy 8:18 says that it is God who gives the ability to become wealthy. In 1 Chronicles 29:12–14, David praised God because "riches and honor" come from Him.

Of course, God is extremely interested in how you acquire your wealth and how you handle it (1 Timothy 6:17). But God does not condemn the legitimate acquisition of wealth. To be poor is not necessarily to be more spiritual. God has no problem with you doing better this year than you did last year.

Observation number two: *God encourages risk-taking*, or to use a more comfortable term, investing. In Matthew 25:14–30, Jesus tells the story of a man who left his money with three of his servants to take out and invest. If you know the story, you know that the master commended the first two servants, who had invested wisely and doubled his money. But think of the risks they must have taken to get that kind of return.

The third servant buried his money. No risk there. He played it absolutely safe, yet the master condemned him, saying, "How dare you take what does not belong to you and not make more with it? The least you should have done was put it in the bank and make me some interest."

Did you know there are many Christians who are not taking legitimate risks? They have never taken the time, talents, and treasure God has given them and maximized these gifts because they are too scared of the risks involved in going all out for Christ. The church needs more legitimate risk-takers.

So God has no problem with wealth and He has no problem with risk-taking per se. Now, let's look at our ten questions and evaluate legitimate gambling versus illegitimate gambling.

The Question of Greed

The first question we need to ask is, Is your risk-taking motivated by greed? Answering this one will go a long way to putting the issue of gambling in proper perspective.

One Sunday a man came to church looking very sad and despondent. The pastor noticed him and asked, "Why are you so sad?"

"Well, two weeks ago my uncle died and left me $75,000. Then a week ago my aunt died and left me $50,000."

The pastor said, "Wait a minute. Two weeks ago your uncle died and left you $75,000. Last week your aunt died and left you $50,000. Why are you so sad?"

The man answered, "Because nobody died this week."

Greed is a consistent desire to have more or demand the best without regard to need. The greedy person sees money as an end in itself. The greedy person always says, "I want more."

The opposite of greed is contentment. First Timothy 6:5b–10 is one of the best statements on greed and contentment in the Bible. Notice verse 6: "Godliness actually is a means of great gain, when accompanied by contentment." Then Paul goes on to explain that when we leave this place, our wallets stay here.

Therefore, a consuming desire to get rich can only lead to "temptation and a snare and many foolish and harmful desires which plunge men into ruin and destruction" (v. 9). Then we read the verse that is so often misunderstood: "For the love of money is a root of all sorts of evil" (v. 10).

Now greed is not necessarily tied to how much you have. You can be rich and greedy, poor and greedy, or middle-class and greedy, because the heart of greed is the desire for more. I don't mean it's wrong to want a better house or a newer car or any of that. But if you cannot be content with where you are until (or unless) God takes you where you want to be, you are greedy.

God condemns greed, the lust for money. People who are greedy are susceptible to get-rich-quick schemes. The Bible clearly condemns such schemes. Proverbs 21:5 says, "The plans of the diligent lead surely to advantage, but everyone who is hasty comes surely to poverty."

Go to Proverbs 28:20: "A faithful man will abound with blessings, but he who makes haste to be rich will not go unpunished." Verse 22 says, "A man with an evil eye hastens after wealth, and does not know that want will come upon him."

You say, "How do I know when I'm being greedy?" Well, let me ask you a couple questions. First, are you pushing even legitimate risks to the point that they become illegitimate? For instance, are you taking unwise business risks in search of that killer deal that will put you on easy street? Perhaps you're pouring more money than you really need to into things like insurance in the hope that if anything happens, you'll clean up. Now these are tough questions, and I can't pretend to answer them for you. But God can show you when you've crossed the line.

If you're either participating in state-sanctioned gambling or you want to, my question is, why do you want to play it? For instance, do you want to play the lottery because you want to contribute to the educational program of your state? Is your motivation to help put more police on the street, or whatever the lottery people say will happen with the money?

Or, do you want to play the lottery because the government has come up with a way for you to get rich quickly? If that is your motivation, then you have forfeited God's biblical means to wealth, because He says that those who participate in get-rich-quick schemes will not go unpunished.

Don't misunderstand. The problem is not being rich. The problem is the greed mentality you used to get there. Now let me ask you something else. Let's say you win twenty million dollars in the lottery. Do you think that winning represents God's plan for your life? Can you honestly say you took that step in obedience to God's leading?

Well, I suppose it is possible. But if you'll pardon the pun, I'll have to say the odds are against it. What I mean is that most people who play the lottery simply grab for the pot of gold because it's there. God's leading or His plan doesn't enter the picture at that particular moment.

What's the problem with that? It means winning the lottery is not tied to anything but a thirst for wealth. It is not tied to God's leading or plan for you. It's not even tied to your needs. So what you are doing is asking God to bless nothingness. You are asking Him to bless getting money for money's sake. That's greed, and God won't bless it.

So let me say it again. If you are not content, then you are driven by greed. I don't mean that you shouldn't want to move forward, but

God wants you to be content where you are until He decides to give you more. And even when it becomes obvious that God does not want you to have more, He still wants you to be content.

As we saw earlier in 1 Timothy 6:10, the love of money is at the root of a lot of other things that can go wrong. If you love money, you will pay a high price for that affection. Many of us have met people who have a lot of money and not much of anything else, including peace of heart.

Maybe you've heard how trappers use rice inside a narrow-necked jar to catch monkeys, or they put shiny aluminum foil in a box covered with a wire mesh to catch raccoons.

The animals reach in and grab what they want, but they can't get their hands out because they are clutching their prize. And they want the stuff so bad that they will sit there stuck and get captured rather than let go and escape.

That's how Satan uses money on us. He gets us squeezing it until we want it so much we are never going to let go. Then he can capture and enslave us.

It's like the businessman who was granted one wish by a genie. He told the genie he wanted to see the stock-market report for a year from that date so he could know ahead of time where to invest and make a killing.

The genie showed the businessman the stock-market report for a year away. At first he was excited, but then he froze in fear. On the other side of the page were the obituaries, and his picture was printed there.

Now that's a fictitious story, but you get the point. Many people have bought houses and are still working on trying to make them homes. Others have bought cars and now they ride in them alone because they have loved money.

You may remember the famous comedian Jack Benny, who was legendary for being a tightwad. They used to tell the joke that one day a man came up to Benny on the street, pointed a gun at him, and said, "Your money or your life."

Benny did not say anything. The thief repeated his demand. "Your money or your life!" Still Benny didn't answer. So the thief said, "What's the matter with you? Didn't you hear me?"

Benny responded, "I'm thinking about it."

Some of us love money that much. We are not sure whether we would rather lose our money or our lives. Is your participation in, or your desire to participate in, any form of gambling based on greed?

The Question of Trust

The second question we need to ask about gambling is this: Is your risk-taking designed to displace God as the supplier of your needs? Or to put it another way, are you using luck to try to replace providence? We are either chancing our way through life or trusting our way through life.

I think there is no question that risks like sound investments, reasonable insurance on our lives and property, and other forms of planning for the future can be legitimate when we treat them as steps of wise stewardship, not as substitutes for our trust in God. A prudent life insurance policy is not an insult to God's faithfulness.

But many people don't need God because they are gambling too hard. Many who play the lottery play it because they have little confidence in God. Proverbs 10:22 says, "It is the blessing of the Lord that makes rich, and He adds no sorrow to it."

Yes, the Devil can also get you rich. But he will make you miserable with your riches. The Lord can make you rich, but "He adds no sorrow to it." With His riches come the riches of life, not just the riches of income or a windfall from gambling.

That's why Psalm 37:7 says to rest in the Lord and wait for Him and don't get frazzled by the prospering of the unrighteous. The issue is not how much you have, but who got it for you. If your confidence in God has been replaced by the hope of a lucky shot in gambling, you have a problem.

Look at Isaiah 65:10: "[The land of] Sharon shall be a pasture land for flocks, and the valley of Achor a resting place for herds, for My people who seek Me." In other words, God is going to bless His people.

Now read verse 11:

> But you who forsake the Lord, who forget My holy mountain, who set a table for Fortune, and who fill cups with mixed wine for Destiny, I will destine you for the sword, and all of you shall bow down to the slaughter. Because I called, but you did not answer; I spoke, but you did not hear. And you did evil in My sight, and chose that in which I did not delight.

Verse 11 is the "wheel of fortune" of the Old Testament. In other words, the people who forsook the Lord had based their lives on luck.

Why does God condemn that? Because it was the pagan way of living. God is the great I Am. He does not operate by luck, and neither should His children. We are to live by His providence, and that is why we operate by planning and prayer, not by chance.

In Matthew 6:19–21, Jesus gives us a very clear and convicting word about wealth:

> Do not lay up for yourselves treasures upon earth, where moth and rust destroy, and where thieves break in and steal. But lay up for yourselves treasures in heaven, where neither moth nor rust destroys, and where thieves do not break in or steal; for where your treasure is, there will your heart be also.

Are you accumulating your treasures with an eternal or an earthly view? That's an important question, because Jesus is saying that your heart always follows your money. Now we would have said it the other way, because it seems as though your money would follow your heart. That is, what you love you'll spend your money on.

But Jesus reversed it because He understood the power of money to wind itself around our hearts. He said what you spend your money on or invest your money in, you will come to love. If you have invested in stocks, for instance, then your heart is going to take you to the *Wall Street Journal*.

Jesus wants us to use our money with an eternal perspective. Why? Because of verse 22:

> The lamp of the body is the eye; if therefore your eye is clear, your whole body will be full of light. But if your eye is bad, your whole body will be full of darkness. If therefore the light that is in you is darkness, how great is the darkness!

In other words, when your eyes go, the rest of you goes. The hands don't know where to touch if the eyes go. The feet don't know where to walk if the eyes go. If the eyes go, the rest of you is in darkness. If you lose divine perspective, if gold replaces God as the trust and guide of your life, you are not only messed up financially, the rest of you goes too.

I once got a firsthand lesson in how this works. I was in the shower when I got soap in my eyes. Well, the first thing I had to do was get a towel. But because I couldn't see, when I reached for the towel I misjudged where I was and hit my head on the top of the soap dish.

Now I couldn't see *and* I had a knot on my head. I also didn't know that the soap had slipped out of the dish. So as I was groping for the door or something to grab hold of, my foot hit the soap. I ended up slipping and sliding all over the shower. Why? Because when my eyes went, I was in trouble.

Jesus says that if you lose divine perspective on money, the rest of you is going to go too, and you will forfeit God's joy and blessing. People who play the lottery don't miss the evening newscast where the winning numbers are given. They are ready for a praise service if they win: "Praise Lotto from whom all blessings flow. Praise Lotto here below!"

Their hope is in the gamble they have made, so their attention—their heart—is there. Has chance replaced God in your risk-taking? If it has, it is illegitimate.

The Question of Productivity

Here's a third question you need to answer: Has your gambling displaced productivity? Are you gambling for things you should work for?

When God made Adam, the first charge He gave him was to be productive. Even in a perfect environment, Adam had a job to do. God's way out of poverty and into financial health is through productivity, not chance. Are you trying to luck your way into things that you should be working productively for?

Paul writes in Ephesians 4:28:

> Let him who steals steal no longer;
> but rather let him labor, performing
> with his own hands what is good, in
> order that he may have something to
> share with him who has need.

Now in order to have something
to share, you have to have something
left over. Paul said one reason for
work is to have something left over to
give. Thus, honest work brings benefit to others as well as oneself. But
what do most people who play the
lottery say? "I sure hope I win so I
won't have to work anymore. The
first thing I'd do if I won is quit my
job, go on a long vacation, and take it
easy the rest of my life."

Wrong! You may not like the job
you have, but that's a different story.
The hope of becoming rich by gambling cannot act as a substitute for
productive labor. That is not what
God had in mind. Remember, Adam
was created perfect in a perfect environment. But even there God gave
His perfect man a perfect job.

Adam only had to do three
things: tend the garden, fellowship
with God, and love Eve. That was the
sum total of his life. From the very
beginning, God prescribed work as
part of His creative order. This is

why you should never help people who don't want to work.

The problem with much of our contemporary welfare system is that it is an incentive not to work. That is what makes welfare wrong. I am not talking about people who can't work. I am talking about people who *won't* work. According to 2 Thessalonians 3:10, if a man won't work don't let him eat. If he comes home saying, "I am hungry," tell him, "Starve." That's what the Scripture says.

God made us to be productive. You say, "But what about investments?" Investments are different, because they have some capability of producing value and therefore the profits are earned. When you make legitimate investments you are investing in something that is productive. It's creating a product or offering a service, producing something of value. The profit comes out of the value.

There's nothing wrong with that because it is part of the mechanism of productivity. God told Adam to plant seeds. He planted seeds even after he and Eve were put out of the garden.

Adam was taking a risk because he did not know whether the ground would produce. But he took the risk, and the seed produced more than what he planted. He always got more out than he put in. He made an investment, and it yielded a profit.

That's the nature of productivity and investment. My question in gambling is, What is your "investment" producing? If it isn't producing anything, then it is an illegitimate risk.

Proverbs 6:9–11 was written by Solomon, a man who would be considered a billionaire by any standards. He knew something about productivity and also the blessing of God. Solomon writes: "How long will you lie down, O sluggard? When will you arise from your sleep? 'A little sleep, a little slumber, a little folding of the hands to rest'—and your poverty will come in like a vagabond, and your need like an armed man." In other words, stop being so lazy. Get up! You can't be sleeping fifteen hours a day and expect luck to bring your ship in. Your ship has sunk. Start being more productive and maybe you will get where you are trying to go.

Proverbs 10:4 says, "Poor is he who works with a negligent hand, but the hand of the diligent makes rich." Look at Proverbs 12:11: "He who tills his land will have plenty of bread, but he who pursues vain things lacks sense." He is silly. Don't play games you can't win, is what he is saying.

If we would develop and use the brains and bodies and talents that God has given us, then we would see how God would bless our productivity. He has no objection to our success, but He doesn't want it to come through chance. He doesn't want it to be motivated by greed. And He doesn't want our *focus* to be on material success, but on the One who may—or may not—give us that material gain.

Instead, He wants riches to come through the productivity of our lives under the hand of a gracious God who can turn things around and make businesses flourish and give us victory where it looks like defeat.

So the issue here is pretty clear. Ask yourself, Am I trying to get all the benefits of productive work without making any effort or investing in any productive work? If all you want to do is have money change hands from the state to you, then you are pursuing an illegitimate hope. An exchange of funds is all that's involved in most gambling.

But what if someone in my church came to me and said, "Pastor, I'm going to play the lottery so I can win and give a lot of money to the church"? Sorry, that would still be an illegitimate approach, an attempt to help God's work through a nonproductive mechanism.

Let me show you one more benefit of productive work. It gives value to money received—a lesson that all our kids need to learn. Kids are born with "give-me-itis." If you give them money long enough, they don't attach any value to what they receive. They think it is all automatic.

My parents used to say, "Do you think money grows on trees?" That's a good question, because evidently kids do think that. How are they going to learn different? Not by watching the significant adults in their lives trying to strike it rich in the lottery!

The Question of Wisdom

The fourth question you need to ask about all risk-taking is, "Am I taking a wise or an unwise risk?"

Wisdom means the ability to make biblically appropriate decisions in the day-to-day issues of life. The Bible often contrasts a wise man and a fool. A fool runs out and does things without planning. A wise man calculates before he makes a decision so he can get maximum productivity from his efforts.

You have one chance in six thousand of being hurt in an automobile crash. You have one chance in half a million of being hurt in an airplane crash—and even that one chance is enough to keep some people from flying. But here in my home state of Texas a person has a one in sixteen million chance of winning the lottery.

Some people go around saying, "Oh yeah, but my number is coming." No. You don't understand. The odds will never get better. If you roll one die, you have one in six chances of rolling a six. If you roll three dice, you have one in 216 chances of rolling three sixes. The more numbers you add, the higher the odds. You won't win.

The gambling folk don't tell you that. What they show you is the person with a $10 million check. People watch and salivate and think, "Lord, have mercy, I could be next!" Of course, that's just what lottery officials want you to think. But is a one-in-sixteen-million chance a wise risk?

I know people who spend $50 a month on the lottery. Over a period of twenty years, that would be a loss of $12,000. And believe me, that money will be lost. You've got a better chance of striking oil in your backyard, or being hit by lightning twice, than you do of winning the lottery.

But if that same $12,000 were invested at 10 percent interest over those twenty years, this person would have $34,365. The wisdom of the two risks pretty well speaks for itself: a guaranteed "O-fer" versus a solid nest egg. Keep in mind also that with legitimate investments, investors receive back more than they put in. Since lotteries are for the benefit of the state, not the participants, the state gives out less than it takes in. Would you be willing to invest in a mutual fund that at the end of each year was consistently worth 80 percent or less of the value it held at the beginning of the year?

In light of this issue of wisdom as applied to gambling, let me give you some biblical guidelines for wise risk-taking. First, you are to take only those risks that meet family needs and further God's work. Jesus says to count the cost before you commit to something (Luke 14:28).

The point I want to make is that when God looks at risk-taking, He's talking about risks that are carefully calculated and weighed. Proverbs 24:3 says that when you take your risk, act on what you know, not what you are guessing about: "By wisdom a house is built, and by understanding it is established." But gambling is a lucky attempt, a shot in the dark.

That is, you ought to act on something you know about or can learn about. You don't throw your life into pure chance. Now let me ask you a question. Suppose you deposited $5,000 in your local bank and the bank agreed to give you 8 percent interest (I said this was make-believe!).

But then suppose the bank's vice president calls you and says, "I've made a decision. In order for the bank to have enough money to pay you 8 percent interest on your $5,000 deposit, we are going to play the lottery today with your money. I believe this is a wise investment move for you, and besides, I just feel like the bank's number is coming up today!"

Would that be OK with you? This bank officer is a proven financial professional, and he really believes the bank's number is coming up. He really believes you are going to win.

However, I suspect you would consider that an unwise risk with your money. In fact, some folk would threaten that bank vice president with legal action if he did something so stupid. Yet when we gamble, we are doing with our money what we would not allow somebody else to do with it, even though our decision is equally unwise.

The Bible says our risk-taking should be based on a plan, not on random, get-rich-quick schemes. Proverbs 3:5 says you should seek divine help and trust in the Lord with all your heart. According to Proverbs

14:15, "The naive believes everything."

Everybody's got a story. Everybody's got a deal, a can't-miss scheme to make you rich with no effort. But something that you can't think through and come to a logical, rational decision about may leave you with empty pockets.

In other words, if you aren't careful you can become what people on the streets call a "sucker," and there truly is one born every minute. In fact, millions of suckers are born every day, because that is exactly what you are when you risk your money on an unplanned, astronomically risky gamble simply because there is a big payday at the end for a few.

Proverbs 15:22 warns us about jumping into a plan without consulting anyone else. If you don't know about it, find somebody who does. Find somebody who knows more than you know so that before you take the risk, you can find out the wisdom of the risk. The question is simple. Is it a wise or unwise risk given the information available?

The Question of Addiction

The fifth of our ten questions about gambling has to do with addiction. Are you becoming addicted to your little gambling thing? Better wake up, because you're a candidate for a *big* gambling thing.

Paul says in 1 Corinthians 6:12, "All things are lawful for me, but not all things are profitable. All things are lawful for me, but I will not be mastered by anything." Anything that becomes an addiction is illegitimate for a Christian to continue doing.

We are not to be addicted or mastered by anything, the apostle says. Compulsive gamblers never started out that way. They started out as casual, recreational gamblers. They did it for fun. It was simply amusement. What's a buck or two a day, after all?

But then the gambling went from being fun to being serious. They had to win. Then it moved from being serious to being a dependency. They found their joy in gambling and were miserable when they were not doing it. Now at the point of compulsiveness they cannot help themselves. They have to gamble.

You may know someone like that. The addictive power of gambling explains why there are more than seven hundred chapters of Gamblers Anonymous today. As gambling operations have proliferated, twelve-step programs for gamblers have proliferated with them.

The gambling problem of baseball player Pete Rose was played out before television cameras for all of us to see. The reason Rose is in the "Hall of Shame" today rather than the Hall of Fame is that he became a compulsive gambler.

Are you addicted to gambling? It doesn't have to be big-time gambling to be addictive. One year we went to the State Fair of Texas, and I decided to play the game where you throw a softball at a pyramid of three milk jugs. I gave the man a dollar, and he gave me a softball. I left one jug standing.

So I thought, "You know, Evans, if you move a little to the left, you can do it." So I gave the man another dollar and fired away. One jug was left standing. I wasn't far enough to the left. That had to be it. I went to my wallet for another dollar. . . .

Ten dollars later, my wife came to get me and said something heavy: "Stop wasting our money." So we left, but I couldn't get that game out of my mind. That softball and jug were messing with my mind. I was sure that jug was loaded with lead or something. I had to go back, so I put my wife on a ride she didn't want to go on so I could go back to that game booth.

My first dollar was just for fun. But by the third or fourth dollar, it had become serious. By the tenth dollar my attitude was, "I'm not going to let them get away with taking ten dollars from me without even a teddy bear to show for it."

See, I had become dependent. I had become compulsive. I'm saying to you it can happen on any level. When you begin to become dependent, the Bible says you are mastered by something other than God. That is addiction, and addiction is a sin that needs to be broken.

So, are you becoming addicted to gambling? Are you finding that you have to do it now, today? Then it's illegitimate.

The Question of Exploitation

Question number six: Is the risk you're taking exploitative in nature? To put it another way, does it require you or someone else to manipulate and use people to pull it off?

The Bible says over and over again that you cannot exploit people to promote your own agenda (see Isaiah 3:14; Amos 4:1–2; Zechariah 7:8–10). Let's consider two of the Ten Commandments God gave Moses in Exodus 20. You know them well: "You shall not steal" and "You shall not covet" (vv. 15, 17). These two commands are also repeated in the New Testament, because they reflect God's unchanging standard.

33

What's the difference between stealing and coveting? Stealing means to take by deceit, stealth, or by force what another person has and thereby bring him under your control. Stealing, in the Old Testament, was more people-focused even though it certainly included property.

Coveting, however, was more property-related. It focused more on the thing rather than on the person, even though you may get the thing from the person. To covet something was to be "thing driven," to greedily seek what someone else owned, to set in motion a way to get something that belonged to someone else.

Now let me show why gambling is exploitative. Let's go back to our whipping boy, the lottery, since it is arguably the most pervasive and frequently used form of gambling by ordinary people.

The lottery is one of the most exploitative gambling mechanisms in existence today. Why? First, because in order for you to win, someone else must lose. When two people sit down to work out an honest business deal, they are looking for a "win/win" situation. If the need is there on one side and the supply of the need is there on the other side, both parties come out winners.

But when the only way I can win is to make you lose, then my desire to win has moved into exploitation. Imagine a business person saying to a potential partner, "I've got a great deal for you. I take all the profits, you take all the losses." Right!

That's the nature of illegitimate gambling, however. You have to take from one to give to another. You have to make many into losers in order to have a handful of winners take everything. Every day, America has megamillions of losers so a few can win. That's exploitation.

It's even worse when you add to this the fact that the lottery is aimed at the poor and financed by the poor. Most lottery outlets are located among the poor. Many people who make $10,000 or less a year spend up to one-fifth of their income on the lottery. If a con man were bilking poor people out of one-fifth of their income, the community would call for his head. But here is the government doing the same thing, and we call it a game. Why does it work so well? Because the people who run lotteries and other gambling enterprises are incredibly slick at selling people an illusion, a dream.

How does it work? Well, what you do is convince this poor man he is never going to get rich by working. He doesn't have any ability. He'll never make anything of himself. He's stuck where he is. He doesn't have the brains or the will to better himself.

But he's got a chance because we've got a game. Why work for it if you can win it? Now you may say, "I don't remember words like that." No, the ads don't say it that way. It's in the impression left behind, the illusion created—and it's so effective and exploitative it's criminal.

To make sure people stay hooked, the lottery's promoters parade some winner in front of the television holding a huge check for four or five million. You don't have to be poor to start salivating when they tell you the next winner could be you.

Here's something else you need to consider. While a dollar or two a day may be soft drink money you'll never even miss, it's really "chump change" because you are helping to support and feed a system that's ripping off poor people.

See, when the poor see this illusion being sold, many of them say, "That's my only hope out of this mess." But every dollar they give to the lottery is a dollar less for food on their table, the rent money, heat in the winter, clothes for their kids. Every time they give a dollar to the lottery, that's one dollar less they have to get out of the situation they are in.

You can't buy an illusion. So when you concoct schemes that create an illusion which takes from the poor, the Bible calls that exploitation. And exploitation, God's Word says, is evil.

Somebody may say, "Wait a minute. Poor people play the lottery voluntarily. Besides, it's legal." But that doesn't make it right. As we all know, legality and morality are often very different things. You have to go beyond what's merely legal and judge these things by a biblical morality.

The big problem with the lottery is it appeals to the weaknesses of people and not to their strengths. It appeals to a person's thoughts of his inability to better himself and his willingness to let the government come in and hand him his future for nothing. So people wait and pray for their big lottery payday while they continue in their circumstances.

The moral law of God says that you and I should not be involved in the exploitation of others, period. That's why you have to understand that the entire system of illegitimate gambling is built on exploitation of people's weaknesses.

We need to appeal to people's strengths. We need to give people hope. We need to train our children in a way that they learn responsibility. If our children are watching us gamble for our future, they are going to learn that gambling is the answer to their future. That's poor training.

We need to tell the poor person to take the money he puts on the lottery and put it into learning a skill so he can earn his way and make a better life for himself. Gambling is exploitation "to the max."

Let me make one more point before we get to our seventh question. There's a lot of talk about taxes these days, what's fair and what isn't fair tax-wise. Well, gambling enterprises like the lottery are actually voluntary regressive taxes. You have to understand that. The government is taxing you when you play.

Now, the government doesn't call it a tax. It calls it a game. But the government is telling us, "We are afraid to tax you because you are going to rebel against that. So we have come up with a way to tax you that you won't fuss about. We are going to make you pay up and think you are having fun doing it. We have created a game in which we will offer you a big payday and make you feel good while we are actually taxing you."

Let me give you the bottom line. There has never been a lottery in the history of America that has raised more money than the government would have raised if that money had been put into productive use in the economy. The lottery is not even a good tax.

The Question of Society

Now we're ready for the seventh question. Does your risk-taking help or hurt society? Paul reminds us, "For not one of us lives for himself, and not one dies for himself" (Romans 14:7).

Obviously, this question is closely related to the previous one. The Bible says in Matthew 5:13–14 that we are to be salt and light. Jeremiah 29:7 says to "seek the welfare of the city." Paul says that government is designed for the common good (Romans 13:4). In other words, a government must ask whether the laws it passes are for the betterment of the people.

When you take a legitimate business risk, you can answer yes to this question. That business is adding something of value to the common good of the American economy. But the twenty billion dollars that organized crime makes each year from gambling are being used to help tear apart the moral fabric of this country.

You must ask, Is my gambling adding to the betterment of my community, or is it adding to the decay and deterioration of the people and

39

environment around me? When a community turns to luck to try to solve its economic problems, it's a sign that that community has lost confidence. People who turn to luck to solve their problems don't have confidence in their abilities anymore.

Luck says you have to turn your life's direction over to random chance. You've got to roll the dice or play the numbers and see what blind fate hands you. Some of the greatest damage that illegitimate risk-taking does is to a person's inner sense of worth and value.

Whenever a man thinks he needs to try his hand in Las Vegas because he is not making it on the job, he has lost confidence in his ability. He does not think much of himself.

Whenever a government must turn to legalized gambling to pay its bills, you know what that government is saying. "We do not have any confidence in our ability to manage growth. We do not have any confidence in our ability to expand the economy by developing businesses, encouraging productivity, and watching our spending. So because we do not have any confidence, we need to play some games."

That's also what churches do that use bingo to raise revenue. Churches are not exempt from this issue. What the church does is say a prayer over it and try to make it look good.

Churches will say they are playing bingo to raise money for the poor and do other good works. But even if they use the money for such causes, I have a question. Why does the church have to resort to games to raise the money it needs? There's only one reason I can think of. It's because the church can't get the people to *give* the money, so it creates a game to get it.

There is nothing wrong with the game of bingo in itself, or even with providing prizes for winners. But something is wrong when a church says by its actions that it doesn't have any confidence that it can move its people to give. What I'm saying is that when you have to resort to gambling in order to meet legitimate needs, you have lost confidence and, therefore, you have hurt the common good.

Gambling, legal and illegal, has led to tax evasion, bribery, swindling, and suicide. Some of us even in the Christian community don't have to look very far to see its results. We can look in our own families and see lives torn apart.

It's hard enough for some people to be happy with the money they make. Add to it the money they are losing on gambling, and you have got a major marital problem. The Bible says that Christians are to overcome evil with good.

It's really critical that we understand that all of this reflects the "devolution," the descent, of a culture. The more gambling proliferates, the more we devolve as a people.

Gambling is just one tentacle of a much larger problem that has wrapped itself around our people, and it's choking us. As long as able-bodied people are looking to the government for their livelihood, our communities will be handicapped.

As I've said before, those who are able to work should be willing to work, and if not, they don't eat. That's not popular, but I'm not trying to be popular or politically correct. I want to be biblically accurate. And this problem grows from generation to generation. The reason we have a spoiled generation is that people want others to do for them what they are responsible to do for themselves.

The government is only responsible to provide a just environment so that you and I have equal access and are not discriminated against based on illegitimate criteria such as race.

Government is responsible for removing tyranny from the marketplace. That's all. But as long as we hand it out, our kids are never going to get up and go get it for themselves. When you cater to weakness, you destroy character. Creating systems that destroy the character of a community is evil.

The Question of Spiritual Effect

In the Bible, money is definitely a spiritual issue. The Bible knows nothing of a two-tiered world where the spiritual and the physical are entirely separate and only the spiritual matters, so it's not important what you do on the physical level. That's Greek philosophy, not biblical theology.

So money is a spiritual issue, because its use or misuse can have spiritual effects. According to the Bible, money is designed to do three basic things: take care of your personal and family needs, further the work of God, and provide help to those who need help, including the poor and oppressed.

So the eighth question we need to ask about using our money in the enterprise called gambling is this: Does it do spiritual harm to others?

I want to do a little extra background on this one because it's important. Let's turn to 1 Corinthians 9:19–22, a key passage where Paul writes of his relationship to unbelievers:

For though I am free from all men, I have made myself a slave to all, that I might win the more. And to the Jews I became as a Jew, that I might win Jews; to those who are under the Law, as under the Law, though not being myself under the Law, that I might win those who are under the Law; to those who are without law, as without law, though not being without the law of God but under the law of Christ, that I might win those who are without law. To the weak I became weak, that I might win the weak; I have become all things to all men, that I may by all means save some.

In other words, Paul did not want to do anything that would keep him from being able to win someone else to Christ. He did not want to hurt his testimony to others, even if he needed to limit his own freedom.

God has given you and me a testimony. So even when it comes to things that we clearly think are OK to do, we must ask if these things are going to hinder our ability to be a witness. Will they hinder anybody from taking us seriously as Christians?

The answer to that is going to vary from place to place. For instance, there are some places I go to minister where it would be illegitimate for me to go to a movie—and

I'm talking about a Walt Disney movie. In that part of the country, Christians don't go to movies. It is an offense to the non-Christian to see a Christian go to movies.

So what would Paul do when he was in those areas? He wouldn't flaunt his freedom. He would avoid the theater because he had a bigger purpose in mind. He didn't want to do anything that hindered him from being a witness.

This not only affects our relationship with unbelievers. In 1 Corinthians 8:13, Paul says, "If food causes my brother to stumble, I will never eat meat again, that I might not cause my brother to stumble." We are not to use our freedom to impede the testimony of Christ, nor are we to cause our brother to stumble. Maybe you see where we're going in terms of gambling.

Your spiritual freedom is a reality, but you can't use your freedom in such a way that you harm another member of God's family. You may ask, "There are so many Christians around with so many different ideas of what's appropriate and what isn't. How can I keep from causing someone to stumble?"

First of all, in order to stumble a person has got to be moving. An individual cannot stumble while he's standing still. What I mean is that

Paul is not talking about offending somebody who just says he is a Christian but who is failing to grow. He is talking about Christians who are trying to grow, and what you are doing is helping to stymie their growth.

There are many things I can't do while I pastor my church in Dallas. Not because these things are wrong, but because weaker Christians would be hindered by them. And so I am limited somewhat by those weaker Christians because I don't want to do anything to harm their spiritual growth.

I have a friend who was ministering in Las Vegas. The church put him up in one of the big hotels. Of course, most of the hotels there are full of casinos. He was staying at such a hotel.

His hosts had arranged to pick him up on Sunday morning for church at about 10:30. He went down to the hotel lobby a few minutes early so he would be ready when they came to pick him up. He looked at his watch and it was about 10:20. So he had ten minutes to wait.

As he stood there waiting, he noticed a slot machine near the front exit. He had always been curious about slot machines. He was watching all these people spend their quarters. He was a preacher, but he was from out of town, so it wasn't as if anyone would know him.

He looked at the slot machine with curiosity, and he decided to go over and put a quarter in it just to satisfy his curiosity. After all, he figured spending a quarter was not really misusing his money. He told me later that he just kind of wanted to do it for the fun of it.

He looked around. He walked outside and looked to make sure no cars were pulling up. He took a quarter out of his pocket and put it in the slot machine. Then he just pulled the handle real fast and looked away.

Problem is, he hit the jackpot! Quarters were coming out everywhere. He was looking all around, catching the quarters. And, of course, while he was catching the quarters, his ride to the church pulled up, and the pastor from the church came inside to pick him up. He has not been invited back.

The point is, we must be sensitive to the cause of Christ. In fact, the more people who will be affected by the choices you make, the more restricted you should be, at least around those people.

One aspect of the spiritual impact of gambling may not have occurred to you, but it's an interesting one: the issue of casting lots in the Bible. Was this a case of God ordering His people to gamble?

Casting lots was sort of like throwing dice. Lots were actually stones in a pouch that would be spun around. Each stone represented a choice in the decision to be made, and the stone that came out indicated the winning choice.

God ordered the lots to be cast on several occasions, but the thing that makes this distinct from our idea of illegitimate risk-taking is that the outcome was in His hands (Proverbs 16:33), not left to blind chance.

In other words, lots were cast to discern the will of God. Whenever God called for the casting of lots, it was because He wanted a decision to be taken out of the hands of men. By controlling the cast, God was making the selection, not men. Of course the people involved in the decision couldn't read God's mind, so they trusted Him to reveal His will through the lot.

So the motivation for the lot was for God to intervene and make the final call. Today we don't need lots. Why? Because God has given the indwelling Holy Spirit to guide every Christian in terms of finding and discovering His will. But the casting of lots brought spiritual benefit, not harm.

And so the question is, will your risk-taking bring spiritual harm to others? You'll notice the question in this section has been broader than the specific issue of gambling, mainly because I wanted you to see the bigger issue involved. This is a question you need to wrestle with long and hard if you're drawn to gambling at all.

The Question of Legitimate Fun

Here is the question a lot of people want to know about. Our ninth concern about gambling is, Can what you want to do be considered legitimate fun? "I only do it for a little fun," a lot of people say about their gambling. "I'm not trying to get rich or make a pile of money so I can quit working and loaf the rest of my life."

It's hard for me to buy this argument with the lottery. There are probably people who get a charge out of scratching game cards with coins, but I doubt if most folk would include that under the category of fun things to do if there weren't the potential of winning a lot of money by doing so.

But let's assume a person gambles strictly for the fun of it, without worrying too much about the payoff. He just likes the thrill of it.

The issue is, How do we know when our fun is legitimate? A lot of things are fun. Eating is fun, and it's legitimate—I hope! But overeating is taking something good and using it for a bad purpose.

Saying that implies a moral standard for fun, doesn't it? Just because something is fun does not make it right. Any moral judgments we make as Christians have to be grounded in God's Word and His character, so let's talk about how God feels about pleasure.

God is into pleasure. God is into fun. The Bible says, for example, that God created everything for His own pleasure (Revelation 4:11). Psalm 35:27 says that God enjoys the prosperity of His people. According to Psalm 149:4, God gets great pleasure out of His people.

Paul says in Ephesians 1:6 that God predestined us to be adopted as His sons because it was the good pleasure of His will to do so. Hebrews 13:12 says that God is pleased when He sees Christian brothers and sisters sharing with one another. God is not against fun.

So if we as Christians are living dull, boring lives, it's not because God has decreed that it should be this way. Some Christians measure the spiritual level of their lives by how successful they are in avoiding anything that might bring them a dash of pleasure.

But an "unfun" Christian life just isn't quite there. Something is missing. If you measure your walk with Christ by how somber it is, then, my friend, you don't know much about God.

In fact, God set a whole day aside for His and man's enjoyment and called it the Sabbath. After God had worked six days in creation, He sat back and rested—not because He was tired, but that He might enjoy His creation. Then God decided, "This is such a good thing to do that I'll share it with My creation."

That's why we should celebrate the Lord's Day every Sunday. The Lord's Day, the Christian Sabbath, is that day set aside for us to enjoy God and His provision. That is what it is supposed to be, a day of enjoyment and rest—a day of legitimate fun, if you will. A day in which you enjoy God in the context of worship and you have fun with His created order.

So if God is not against fun, the question we have to ask is when our fun is legitimate. Look at Ecclesiastes 5:18: "Here is what I have seen to be good and fitting: to eat, to drink and enjoy oneself in all one's labor in which he toils under the sun during the few years of his life which God has given him; for this is his reward."

God's reward for you as His child is that you might enjoy His provisions. In the few years you have here on earth, God says to you, "I want you to enjoy your labor and its fruit." So you ought to do things well. Work hard and play hard. If you love your job, you should love the fruit of your job as much as you love your job.

Let's look at 1 Timothy 6:17:

> Instruct those who are rich in this present world not to be conceited or to fix their hope on the uncertainty of riches, but on God, who richly supplies us with all things to enjoy.

If God has given you money and you are honoring Him with the money you have, taking care of your family, and giving as you should, then if He gives you a little extra and you want to have fun with the extra in a way that does not dishonor Him, God says He has given you that extra to enjoy.

Don't let other people make you feel guilty for enjoying it either. Don't let people make you feel bad about the house you can afford to live in or the car you can afford to drive or the clothes you can afford to wear, as long as you are not compromising your spiritual priorities to enjoy these things or being selfish with God's provisions.

If God is not against fun, and if He even supplies us extra sometimes just for our enjoyment, how does this relate to the fun argument for gambling?

Well, simply this. God is against any form of fun that elevates the love of pleasure over love for Him. In 2 Timothy 3:4 Paul speaks of those people who in the last days will be marked by many things, among which is that they will be "lovers of pleasure rather than lovers of God." I think we're seeing this fulfilled today.

Applying this to gambling means you have to answer the question of whether your desire to participate in any form of gambling has grown to the point where it is pushing aside your love for God. It's amazing how many Christians will give a lot of energy to fun and little energy to worship. If you love your fun more than you love your Lord, your priorities are out of order, and even legitimate risk-taking has become illegitimate.

So the question we have to ask about gambling, or any fun for that matter, is this: Are you deriving more pleasure from this activity than you are from your relationship to God? If so, you have a spiritual problem on your hands.

The next question you have to answer about fun is the one we asked above, the issue of whether the activity you want to do is harmful to others. Does it violate any of the other guidelines we are discussing?

If not, and if you can enjoy it knowing God is present, then He has no problem with your risk-taking fun. That does not mean we have a license for nonstop fun. Putting limitations on our leisure activities is part of the discipline of the Christian life.

For instance, when you teach a teenager how to drive, he sees it as fun. But you get real serious about his fun, because you want to keep him alive so he can enjoy the fun of driving. To do that, you have to put serious limits on what he may consider the fun parts of driving, such as speeding.

Kids often think the job of adults on this earth is to kill their fun. But I don't want to kill my kids' fun. I just don't want their fun to kill them! Restrictions on fun are necessary and normal.

So even if after all this you can still see your way clear to participate in certain forms of gambling, you are not free to gamble as much as you may like.

The Question of Stewardship

This tenth and final question may be the most important of all. Is gambling good stewardship?

To be a steward means that you are a manager of somebody else's property. You own nothing. When my wife and I were in seminary, we used to house-sit for income. People who were going on vacation would call Dallas Seminary for the name of a seminary student or couple who would come to stay in their home and keep an eye on things.

When Lois and I stayed at someone's home, we were the stewards of the home. We got full run of the home. We could eat the food, cook on the stove, sleep in the bed. Sometimes we would stay in a home in the posh section of Dallas. I knew that I would never get there again, so I maxed that baby out. Sometimes we invited people over.

It was magnificent, but my wife would always remind me that this was not our house. We could use it, but it belonged to someone else. We were just the caretakers.

You and I are merely stewards of everything we have. The Bible says it's all on loan. We came into this world with nothing, and we are leaving here the same way. The only reason we are not going to go out naked is that somebody else will dress us.

The Bible says you will leave with exactly nothing. Hearses don't pull U-Hauls. You take nothing with you. The moment you lose sight of the fact that you are only a steward— a manager—of God's stuff, you are headed for problems.

The moment you start walking around God's creation like you own it, He is going to let you know this is not your home. Many of us act like what we have is "Mine, mine, mine."

No, no, no. It is just ours to manage. It is not ours to own. If we don't have this view of stewardship, we make God the visitor and us the owner, and God is not into that. That's why the Bible says we lose our blessing. Many of our prayers will not be answered because we want to own it. We want to control it.

The beautiful thing about having someone else own something is that when it breaks, the owner has to fix it. If you let God own your life, when it breaks down He has to fix it. When you let Him own you and own your money, when the money runs out, He has to supply it.

As long as it is your money and your house and your car, when it breaks, you get to fix it. That is what God says in Malachi 3. God is saying, "You're robbing Me of My tithes and offerings, so therefore, I will let the locusts come and destroy you."

The greatest story of biblical Christianity in the history of America is the African-American church under slavery. There were no government or social support systems, no federal grants, no welfare systems. Yet without any of that, my ancestors not only carved out a religious order, but also banks, legal firms, family support systems, surrogate parenting, and social movements.

My ancestors did all of that without any government support. We have all of this government and social support today, and we are still losing ground. The problem is we have replaced dependence on God with dependence on the government, an illegitimate mind-set that continues to have devastating effects on our communities. When you put God in His rightful place, He can help you meet any legitimate need you may have. We have got to be better stewards.

The application of stewardship to gambling involves answering the question, Do I believe God has provided me with a certain amount of money for the express intention of wagering it so He can get the glory and benefit if I win? I realize I tilted the question a little, but the concept is valid.

See, up to now we've been concerned primarily with whether gambling is something God would object to. But the issue of stewardship says that God is not just a passive observer in gambling, He must actually be bankrolling me since everything I have belongs to Him.

My money is really His money, so I have to believe it's OK with Him to risk it if I believe at all in the teaching of stewardship. Gambling becomes bad stewardship when it suggests that God is so tight with His money that I can't trust Him to meet my needs on His own, and I need to help Him along by going for a lucky strike.

God wants you to seek His kingdom above all, and He will take care of the needs you're trying to meet through your own schemes. When you look for all these other things and skip over His kingdom, then He leaves you on your own.

If we only knew about God what He knows about Himself, we not only could afford to be generous stewards, but we would also limit our risk-taking to those areas that would glorify God.

So what is the bottom line? Not all gambling or risk-taking is wrong. But any form of gambling that violates any of the ten questions above is certainly a bad bet!

What Is The Urban Alternative?

The Urban Alternative (TUA) is a ministry designed to equip, unite, and empower the church to impact individuals, families, and communities for the rebuilding of their cities from the inside out. TUA believes that the Bible has practical answers for all of life's issues we face.

TUA's program includes a two-minute and thirty-minute daily radio broadcast, as well as a thirty-minute weekly TV broadcast, where Dr. Evans provides God's answers to the issues that people face today. TUA also provides audio, video, and written resources for spiritual development and community impact. In addition, TUA hosts an annual National Church Development Conference designed to assist pastors and church leaders in expanding this influence in the lives of their members, as well as in the broader communities in which they are situated.

TUA's comprehensive, biblically-based community development program is called Project Turnaround.

Included in Project Turnaround are strategic impacts addressing the areas of church development, youth and family, economic development, housing, health and education, and community mobilization and reconciliation. TUA believes that the church and not the government can provide the best plan for changing our communities.

For a free TUA newsletter and resource catalog, please contact:

The Urban Alternative
P.O. Box 4000
Dallas, TX 75208
1–800–800–3222

Moody Press, a ministry of the Moody Bible Institute, is designed for education, evangelization, and edification. If we may assist you in knowing more about Christ and the Christian life, please write us without obligation: Moody Press, c/o MLM, Chicago, Illinois 60610.